WORLD'S GREATEST HYMNS
FOR PIANO & VOICE

70 OF THE MOST INSPIRATIONAL MELODIES
Suitable for Solo Piano Performance
or as an Accompaniment
Includes Vocal Line, Lyrics and Guitar Chords

Selected and Arranged by
JERRY RAY

World's Greatest Hymns includes the most cherished and beloved hymns of the church. We have selected hymns of praise and celebration, songs of inspiration and worship, plus contemporary titles that communicate faith, hope and confidence.

Each piece has been arranged in a very accessible approach and uniquely features:

- a two- or four-bar introduction in the same style as the hymn setting
- a vocal line for solo or group singing
- up to three verses of lyrics
- a first and second ending with an appropriate "turnaround," plus a third ending to complete the arrangement
- guitar chords and dynamics
- a piano part that is complete in itself for solo performance

It is my desire that the beautiful melodies and powerful lyrics contained in *World's Greatest Hymns* will inspire, encourage and help strengthen your daily walk. Martin Luther certainly parallels our motives behind providing you with such a unique and complete collection of the *World's Greatest Hymns*:

> "Next to the Word of God, music deserves the highest praise.
> The gift of language combined with the gift of song was given to
> man that he should proclaim the Word of God through music."

Sing On!

Jerry Ray

Second Edition
Copyright © MMII by Alfred Publishing Co., Inc.
All rights reserved. Printed in USA.

Music engraving: Nancy Butler

Alfred

Contents

In Christ There Is No East or West

Words by John Oxenham

Music by Alexander R. Reinagle
Arranged by Jerry Ray

A Mighty Fortress Is Our God

Words by Martin Luther
Based on Psalm 46

Music by Martin Luther
Arranged by Jerry Ray

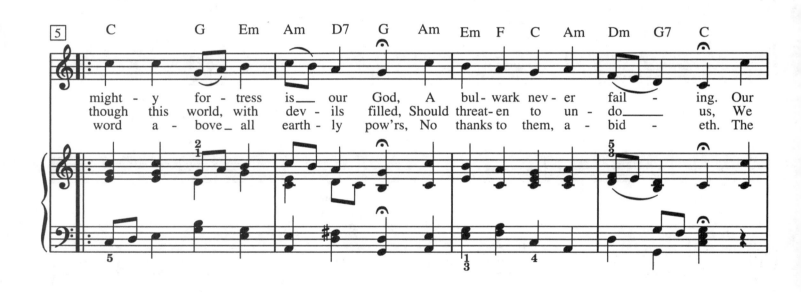

might - y for - tress is___ our God, A bul - wark nev - er fail - ing. Our
though this world, with dev - ils filled, Should threat-en to un - do___ us, We
word a - bove__ all earth - ly pow'rs, No thanks to them, a - bid - eth. The

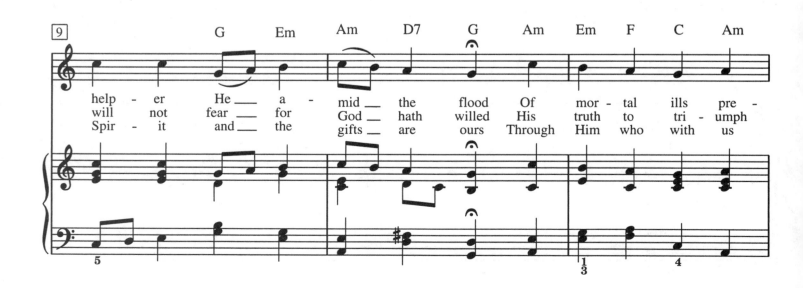

help - er He ___ a - mid ___ the flood Of mor - tal ills pre -
will not fear ___ for God ___ hath willed His truth to tri - umph
Spir - it and ___ the gifts ___ are ours Through Him who with us

Come, Thou Almighty King

Text source unknown

Music by Felice de Giardini
Arranged by Jerry Ray

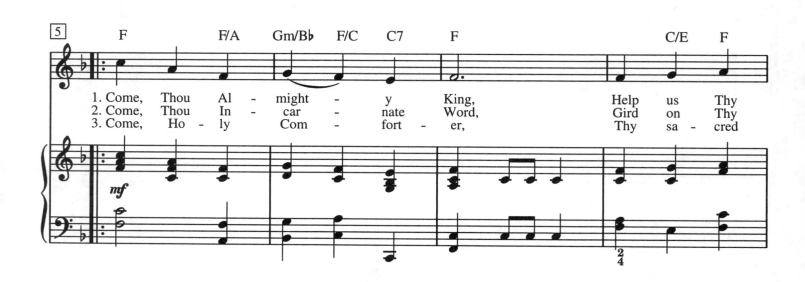

1. Come, Thou Al - might - y King, Help us Thy
2. Come, Thou In - car - nate Word, Gird on Thy
3. Come, Ho - ly Com - fort - er, Thy sa - cred

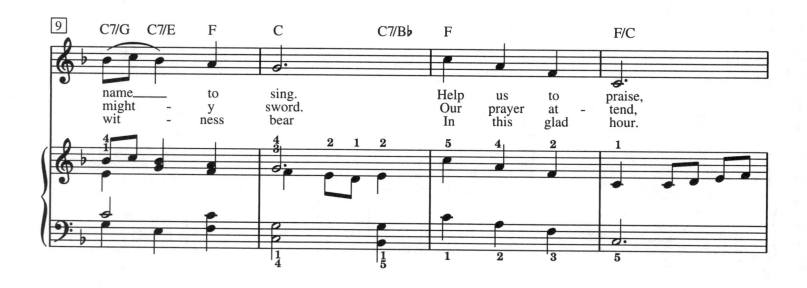

name____ to sing. Help us to praise,
might - y sword. Our prayer at - tend,
wit - ness bear In this glad hour.

I Know Whom I Have Believed

Words by Daniel W. Whittle

Music by James McGranahan
Arranged by Jerry Ray

Christ the Lord Is Risen Today

Words by Charles Wesley

Music from *Lyra Davidica*
Arranged by Jerry Ray

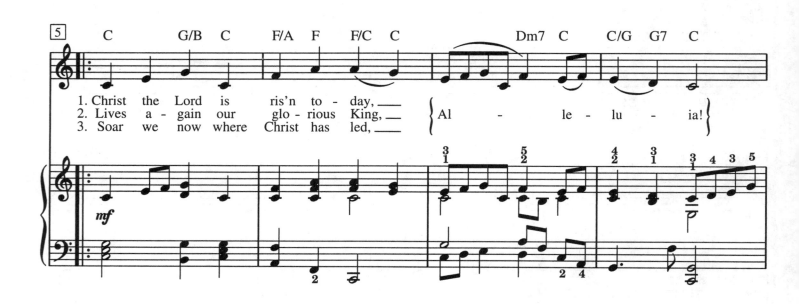

1. Christ the Lord is ris'n to-day, ___ Al - le - lu - ia!
2. Lives a - gain our glo - rious King, ___
3. Soar we now where Christ has led, ___

Sons of men and an - gels say: ___ Al - le - lu - ia!
Where, O death, is now thy sting? ___
Fol - l'wing our ex - alt - ed Head, ___

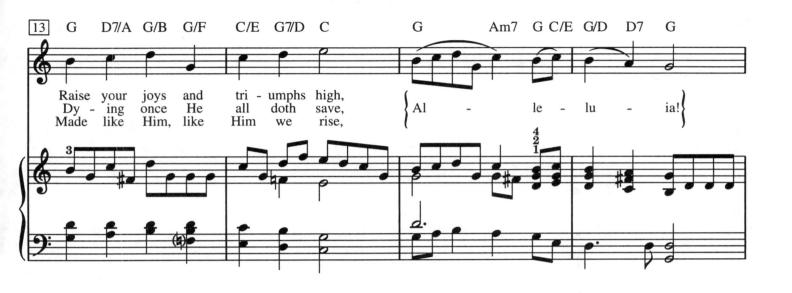

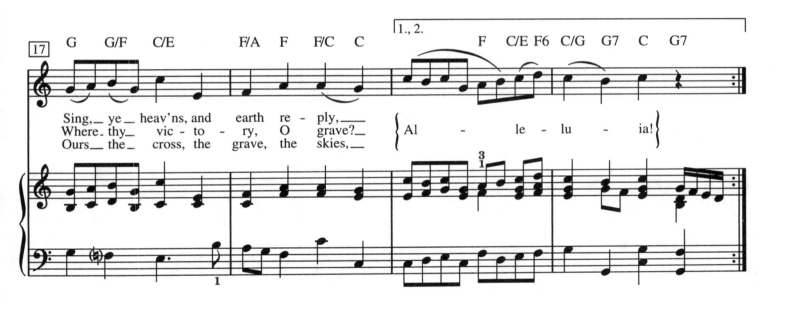

Abide with Me

Words by Henry F. Lyte

Music by William H. Monk
Arranged by Jerry Ray

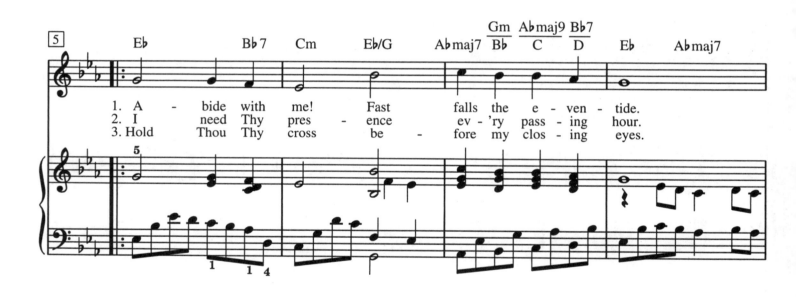

1. A - bide with me! Fast falls the e - ven - tide.
2. I need Thy pres - ence ev - 'ry pass - ing hour.
3. Hold Thou Thy cross be - fore my clos - ing eyes.

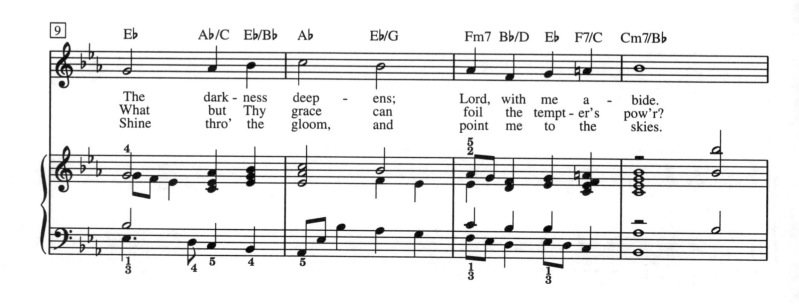

The dark - ness deep - ens; Lord, with me a - bide.
What but Thy grace can foil the tempt - er's pow'r?
Shine thro' the gloom, and point me to the skies.

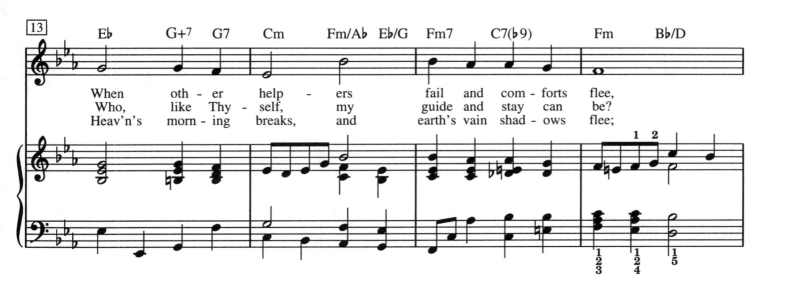

When oth - er help - ers fail and com - forts flee,
Who, like Thy - self, my guide and stay can be?
Heav'n's morn - ing breaks, and earth's vain shad - ows flee;

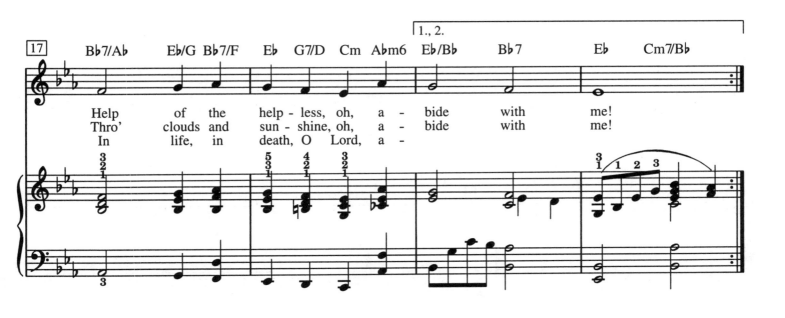

Help of the help - less, oh, a - bide with me!
Thro' clouds and sun - shine, oh, a - bide with me!
In life, in death, O Lord, a -

bide with me! _____

Crown Him with Many Crowns

Words by Matthew Bridges

Music by George J. Elvey
Arranged by Jerry Ray

1. Crown Him with man - y crowns, The Lamb up - on His throne. Hark,
2. Crown Him the Son of God, Be - fore the worlds be - gan, And
3. Crown Him the Lord of love! Be - hold His hands and side, Rich

how the heav'n - ly an - them drowns All mu - sic but its own! A-
ye who tread where He hath trod, Crown Him the Son of Man. Who
wounds yet vis - i - ble a - bove, In beau - ty glo - ri - fied. All

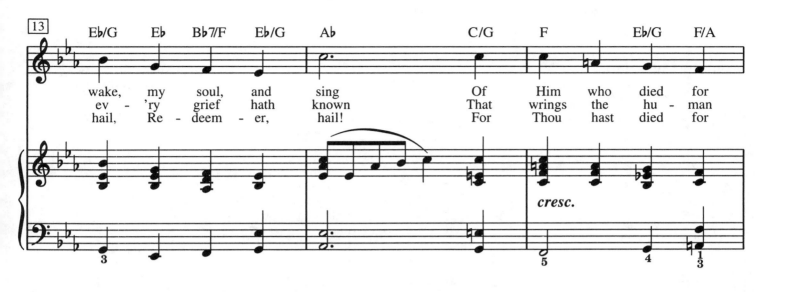

God Will Take Care of You

Words by Civilla D. Martin

Music by W. Stillman Martin
Arranged by Jerry Ray

Not too fast

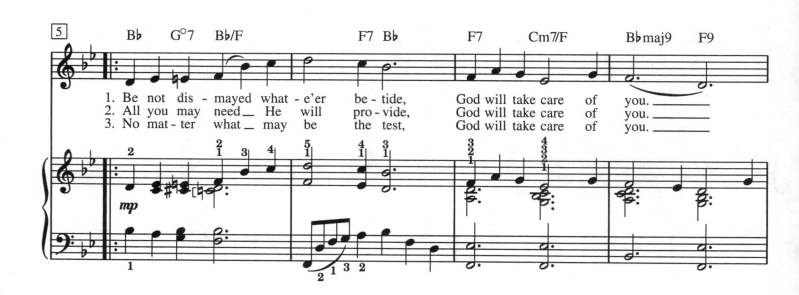

1. Be not dis-mayed what-e'er be-tide, God will take care of you.
2. All you may need He will pro-vide, God will take care of you.
3. No mat-ter what may be the test, God will take care of you.

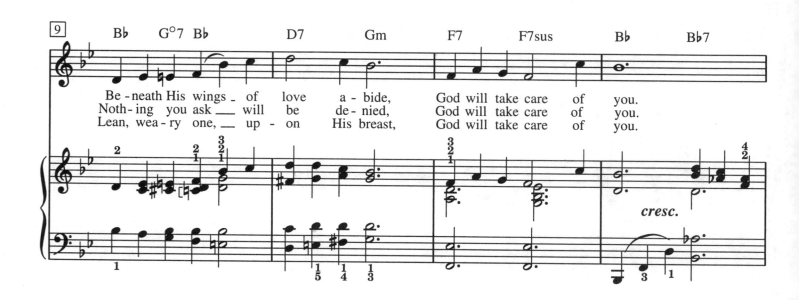

Be-neath His wings of love a-bide, God will take care of you.
Noth-ing you ask will be de-nied, God will take care of you.
Lean, wea-ry one, up-on His breast, God will take care of you.

I Need Thee Every Hour

Words by Annie S. Hawks
and Robert Lowry

Music by Robert Lowry
Arranged by Jerry Ray

1. I

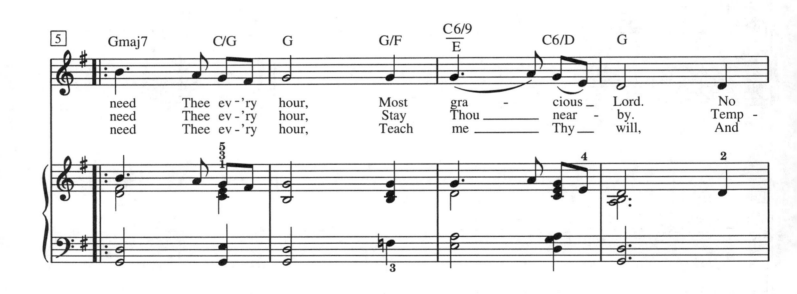

| Gmaj7 | C/G | G | G/F | C6/9 / E | C6/D | G |

need Thee ev-'ry hour, Most gra - cious Lord. No
need Thee ev-'ry hour, Stay Thou near - by. Temp -
need Thee ev-'ry hour, Teach me Thy will, And

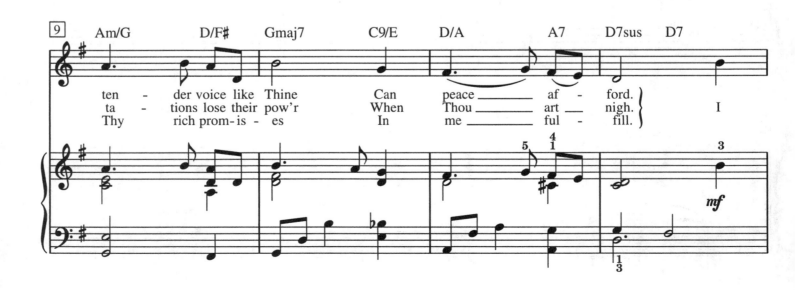

| Am/G | D/F# | Gmaj7 | C9/E | D/A | A7 | D7sus | D7 |

ten - der voice like Thine Can peace af - ford.
ta - tions lose their pow'r When Thou art nigh. I
Thy rich prom-is - es In me ful - fill.

All Hail the Power of Jesus' Name

Words by Edward Perronet

Music by Oliver Holden
Arranged by Jerry Ray

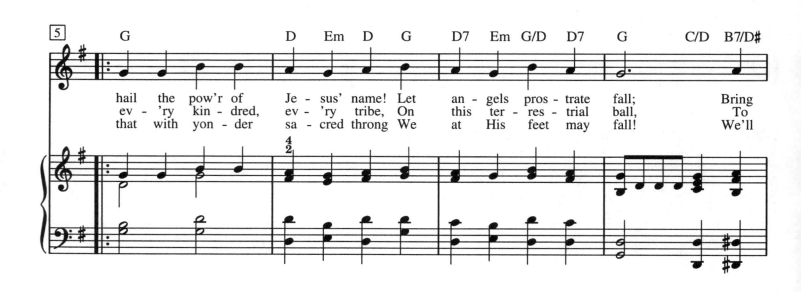

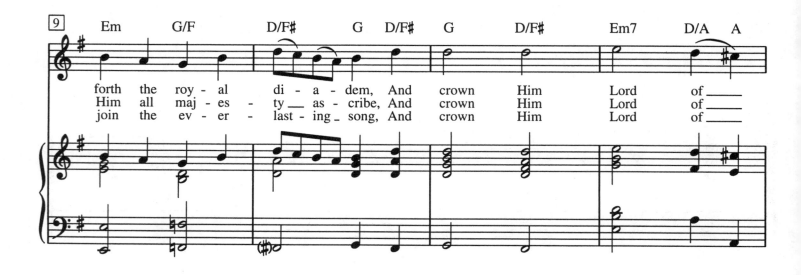

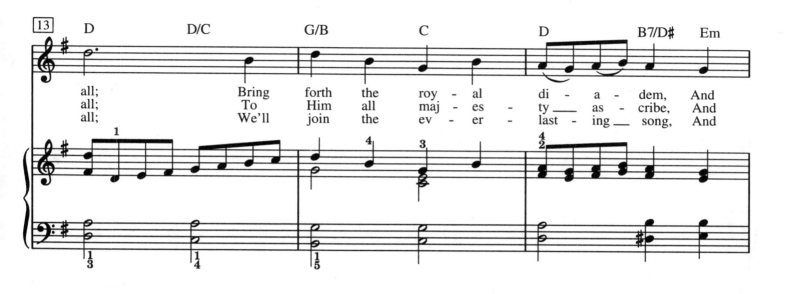

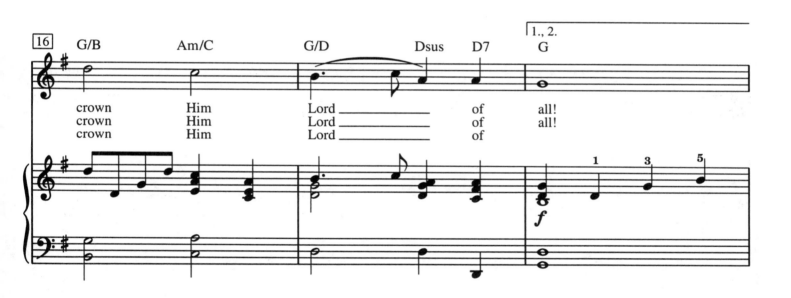

The Church's One Foundation

Words by Samuel J. Stone

Music by Samuel S. Wesley
Arranged by Jerry Ray

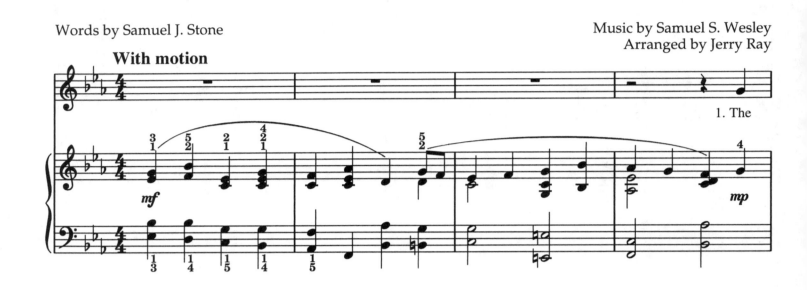

Church-'s one foun - da - tion Is Je - sus Christ her Lord. She
lect from ev - 'ry na - tion, Yet one o'er all the earth. Her
toil and trib - u - la - tion And tu - mult of her war, She

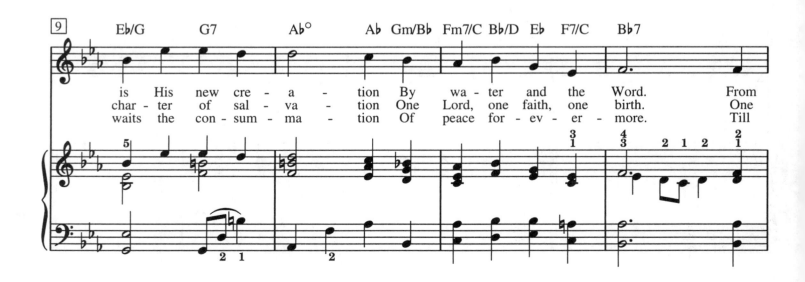

is His new cre - a - tion By wa - ter and the Word. From
char - ter of sal - va - tion One Lord, one faith, one birth. One
waits the con - sum - ma - tion Of peace for - ev - er - more. Till

I Surrender All

Words by Judson W. Van DeVenter

Music by Winfield S. Weeden
Arranged by Jerry Ray

Moderately slow

1. All to Je - sus I sur - ren - der, All to Him I free - ly give.
2. All to Je - sus I sur - ren - der, Hum - bly at His feet I bow.
3. All to Je - sus I sur - ren - der, Lord, I give my - self to Thee.

I will ev - er love and trust Him, In His pres - ence dai - ly live.
Word - ly pleas - ures all for - sak - en, Take me, Je - sus, take me now.
Fill me with Thy love and pow - er, Let Thy bless - ing fall on me.

Fairest Lord Jesus

Anonymous

Crusader's Hymn
Arranged by Jerry Ray

Tenderly

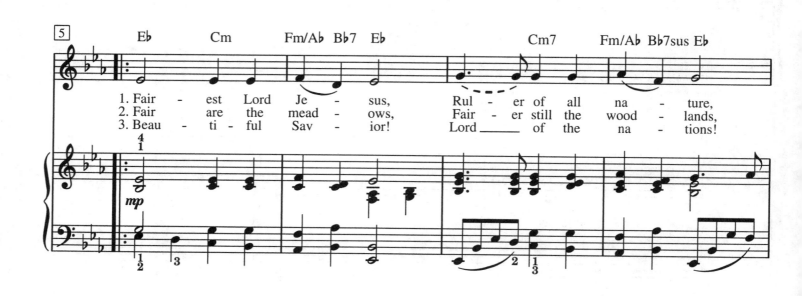

1. Fair - est Lord Je - sus, Rul - er of all na - ture,
2. Fair are the mead - ows, Fair - er still the wood - lands,
3. Beau - ti - ful Sav - ior! Lord of the na - tions!

O Thou of God and man the Son.
Robed in the bloom - ing garb of spring.
Son of God and Son of Man!

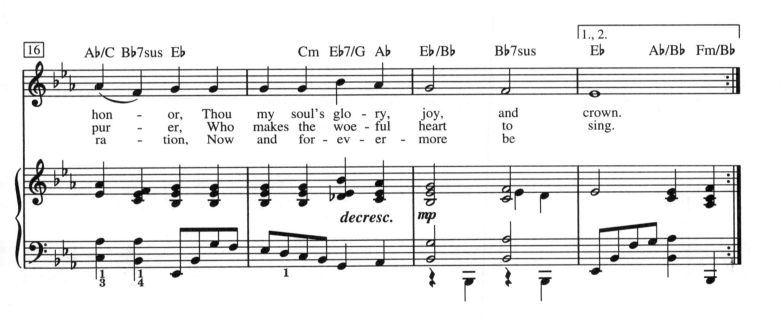

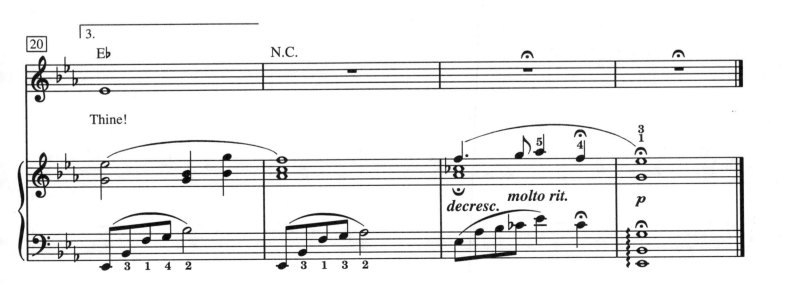

Holy, Holy, Holy

Words by Reginald Heber

Music by John B. Dykes
Arranged by Jerry Ray

Majestically

1. Ho - ly, ho - ly, ho - ly! Lord God Al - might - y!
2. Ho - ly, ho - ly, ho - ly! all the saints a - dore Thee,
3. Ho - ly, ho - ly, ho - ly! Lord God Al - might - y!

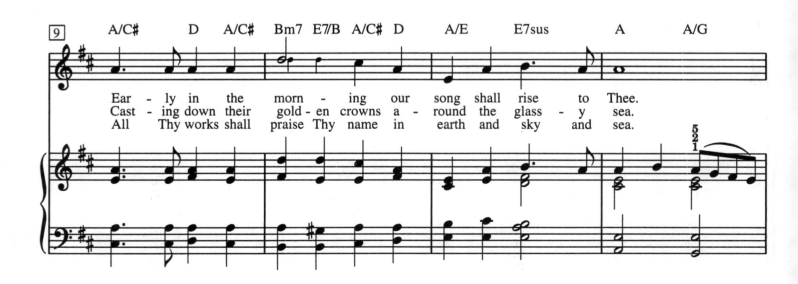

Ear - ly in the morn - ing our song shall rise to Thee.
Cast - ing down their gold - en crowns a - round the glass - y sea.
All Thy works shall praise Thy name in earth and sky and sea.

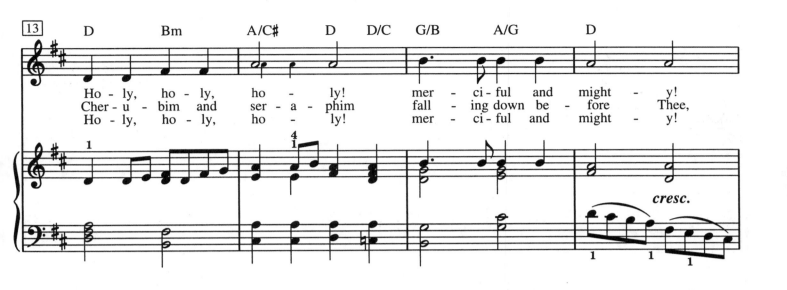

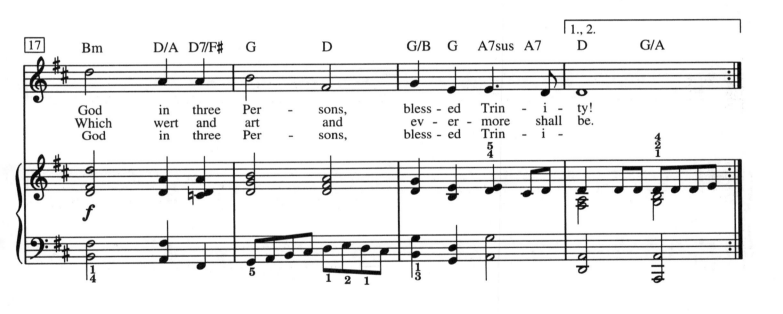

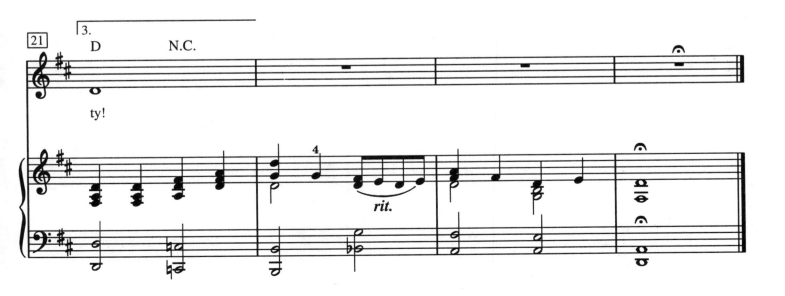

All the Way My Savior Leads Me

Words by Fanny J. Crosby

Music by Robert Lowry
Arranged by Jerry Ray

Jesus Loves Me

Words by Anna B. Warner

Music by William B. Bradbury
Arranged by Jerry Ray

Amazing Grace

Words by John Newton
and John P. Rees

Traditional
Arranged by Jerry Ray

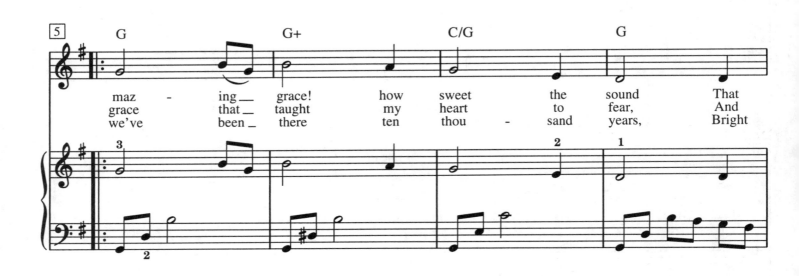

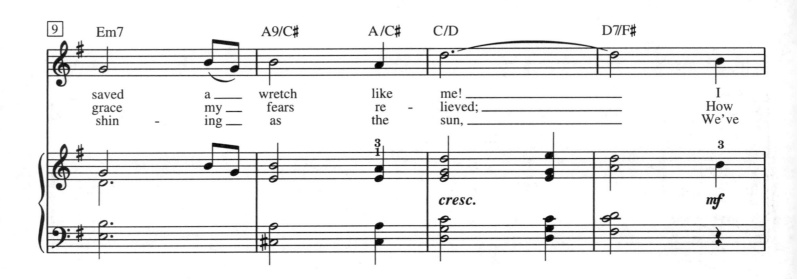

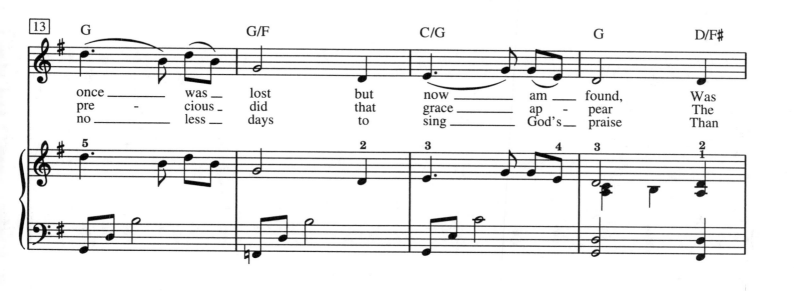

once _____ was __ lost but now _____ am __ found, Was
pre - cious __ did that grace _____ ap - pear The
no _____ less __ days to sing _____ God's __ praise Than

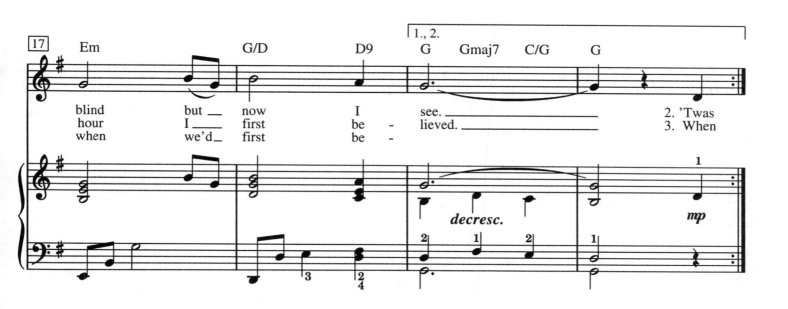

blind but __ now I see. _____ 2. 'Twas
hour I __ first be - lieved. _____ 3. When
when we'd __ first be -

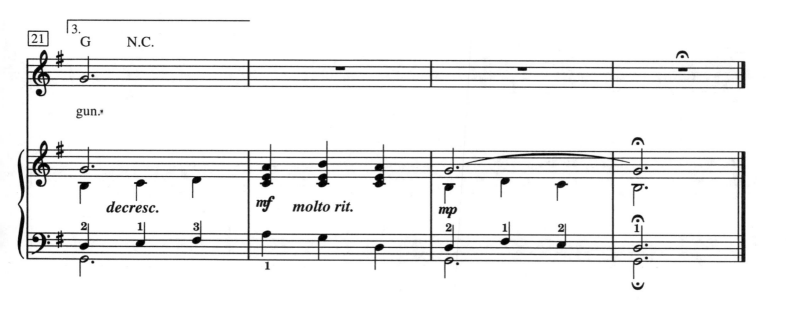

gun.

Leaning on the Everlasting Arms

Words by Elisha A. Hoffman

Music by Anthony J. Showalter
Arranged by Jerry Ray

1. What a fel - low-ship, what a joy di - vine,
2. O how sweet to walk in this pil - grim way,
3. What have I to dread, what have I to fear,

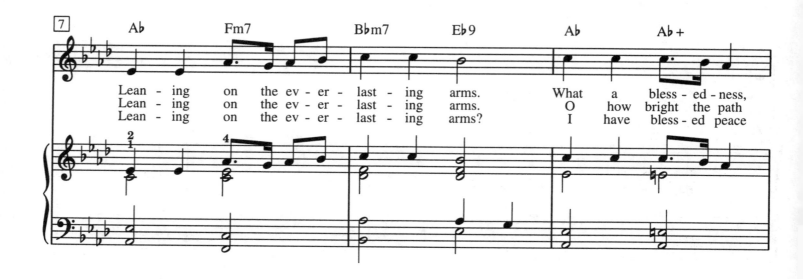

Lean - ing on the ev - er - last - ing arms. What a bless - ed - ness,
Lean - ing on the ev - er - last - ing arms. O how bright the path
Lean - ing on the ev - er - last - ing arms? I have bless - ed peace

Only Trust Him

Words by John H. Stockton

Music by John H. Stockton
Arranged by Jerry Ray

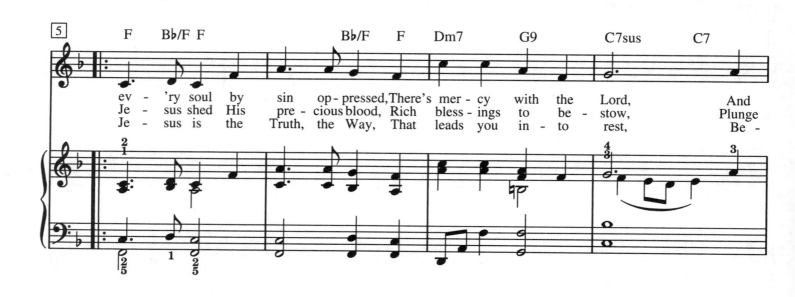

Savior, Like a Shepherd Lead Us

Words by Dorothy A. Thrupp

Music by William B. Bradbury
Arranged by Jerry Ray

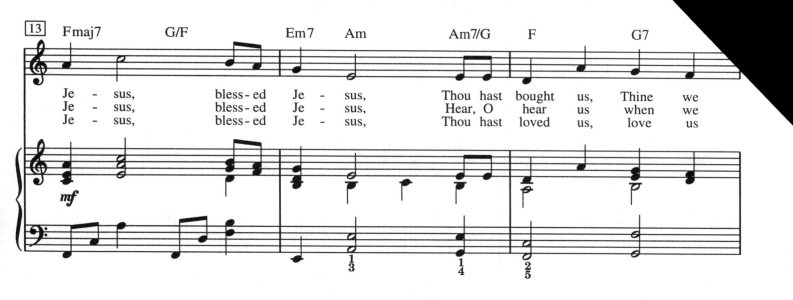

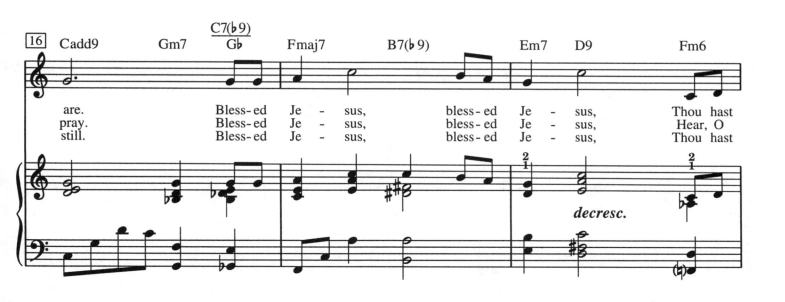

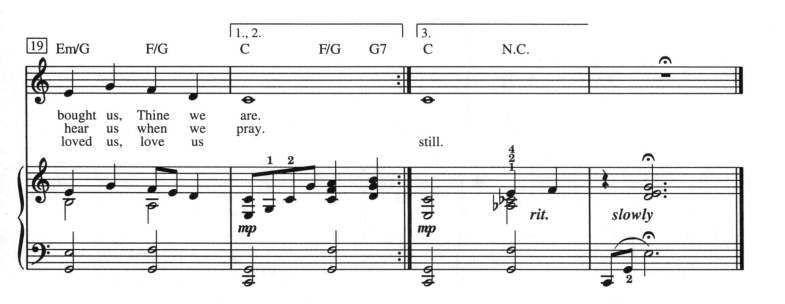

'Tis So Sweet to Trust in Jesus

. R. Stead

Music by William J. Kirkpatrick
Arranged by Jerry Ray

1. 'Tis so sweet to trust in Je - sus, Just to take Him at His word.
2. Yes, 'tis sweet to trust in Je - sus, Just from sin and self to cease.
3. I'm so glad I learned to trust Him, Pre - cious Je - sus, Sav - ior, Friend.

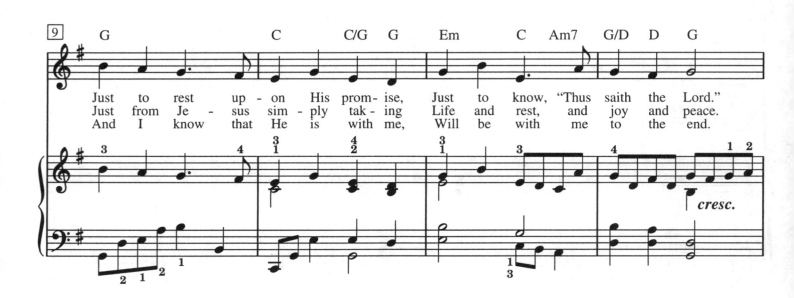

Just to rest up - on His prom - ise, Just to know, "Thus saith the Lord."
Just from Je - sus sim - ply tak - ing Life and rest, and joy and peace.
And I know that He is with me, Will be with me to the end.

When We All Get to Heaven

Words by Eliza E. Hewitt

Music by Emily D. Wilson
Arranged by Jerry Ray

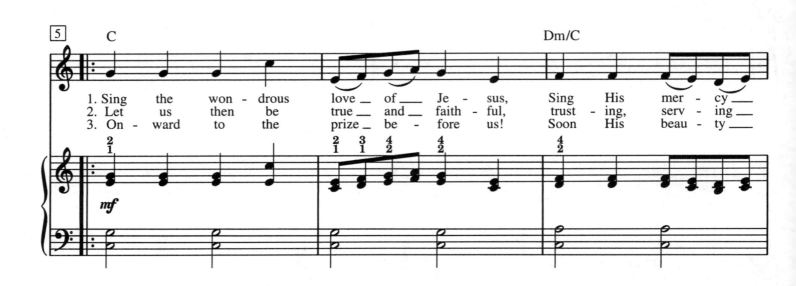

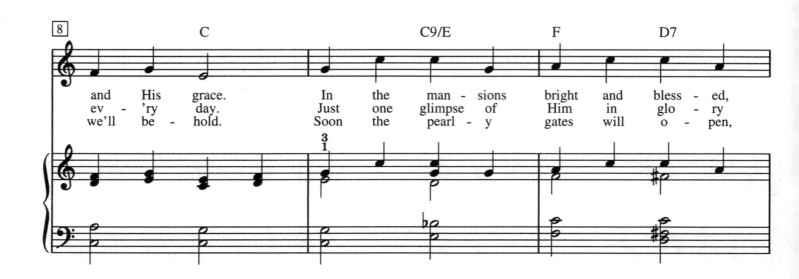

Faith of Our Fathers

Words by Frederick W. Faber

Music by Henry F. Hemy
Arranged by Jerry Ray

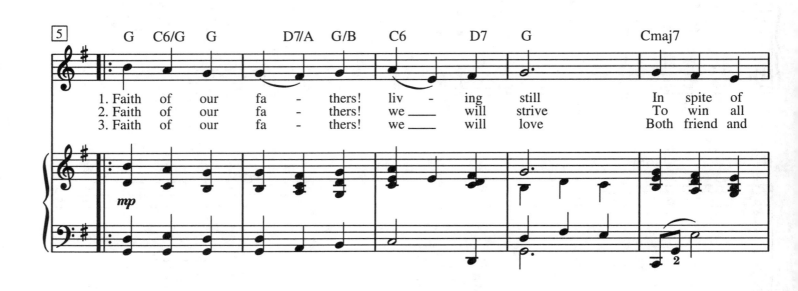

1. Faith of our fa - thers! liv - ing still In spite of
2. Faith of our fa - thers! we will strive To win all
3. Faith of our fa - thers! we will love Both friend and

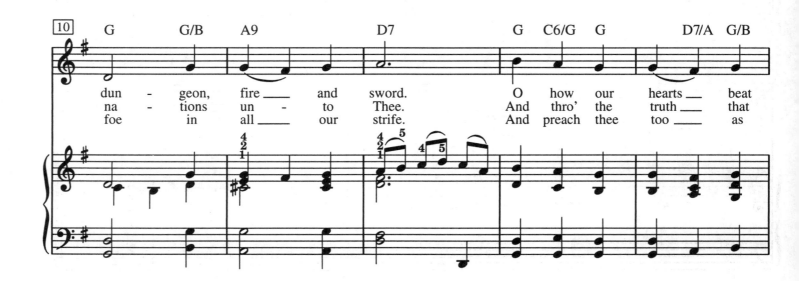

dun - geon, fire and sword. O how our hearts beat
na - tions un - to Thee. And thro' the truth that
foe in all our strife. And preach thee too as

Day by Day

Words by Carolina Sandell-Berg

Music by Oscar Ahnfelt
Arranged by Jerry Ray

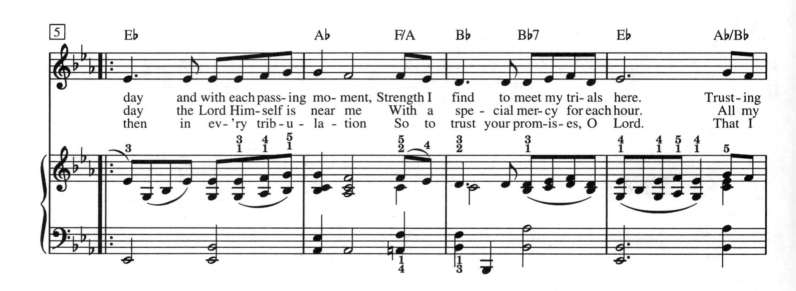

day   and with each pass-ing mo-ment, Strength I find   to meet my tri-als here.   Trust-ing
day   the Lord Him-self is near me   With a spe-cial mer-cy for each hour.   All my
then   in ev-'ry trib-u- la-tion   So to trust your prom-is-es, O Lord.   That I

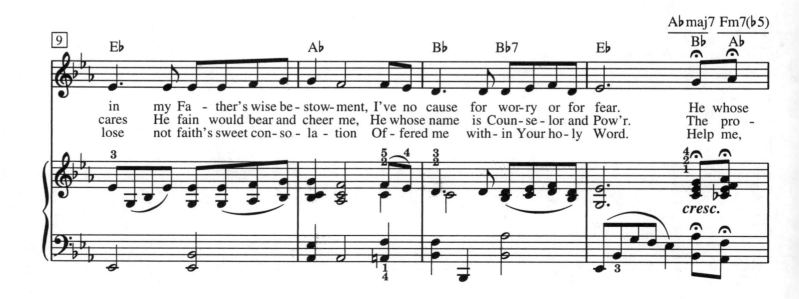

in   my Fa-ther's wise be-stow-ment, I've no cause for wor-ry or for fear.   He whose
cares   He fain would bear and cheer me, He whose name is Coun-se-lor and Pow'r.   The pro-
lose   not faith's sweet con-so-la-tion Of-fered me with-in Your ho-ly Word.   Help me,

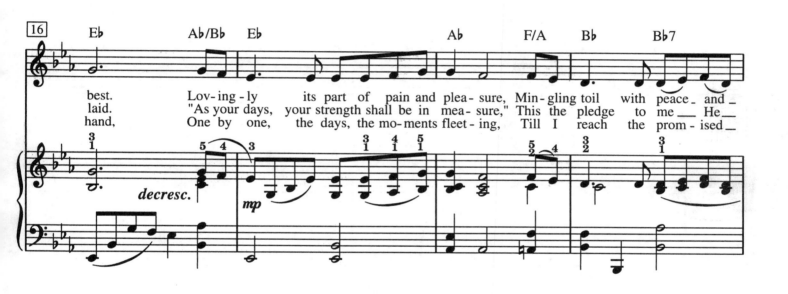

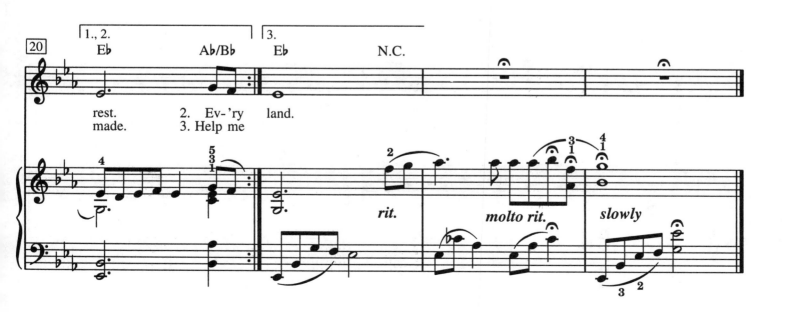

Shall We Gather at the River?

Words by Robert Lowry

Music by Robert Lowry
Arranged by Jerry Ray

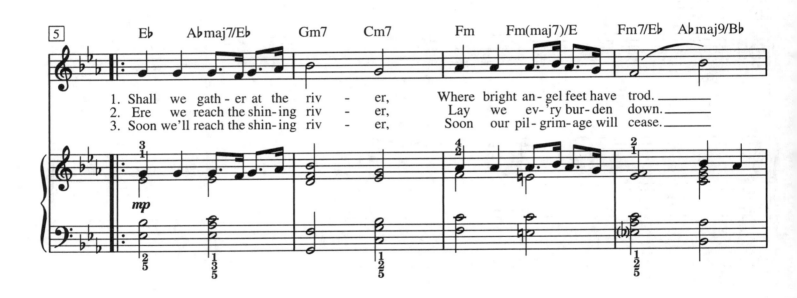

1. Shall we gath-er at the riv - er, Where bright an-gel feet have trod.
2. Ere we reach the shin-ing riv - er, Lay we ev-'ry bur-den down.
3. Soon we'll reach the shin-ing riv - er, Soon our pil-grim-age will cease.

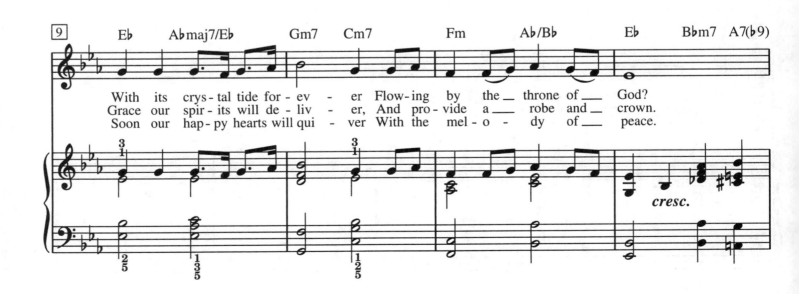

With its crys-tal tide for - ev - er Flow-ing by the __ throne of __ God?
Grace our spir - its will de - liv - er, And pro - vide a __ robe and __ crown.
Soon our hap - py hearts will qui - ver With the mel - o - dy of __ peace.

Take the Name of Jesus with You

Words by Lydia Baxter

Music by William H. Doane
Arranged by Jerry Ray

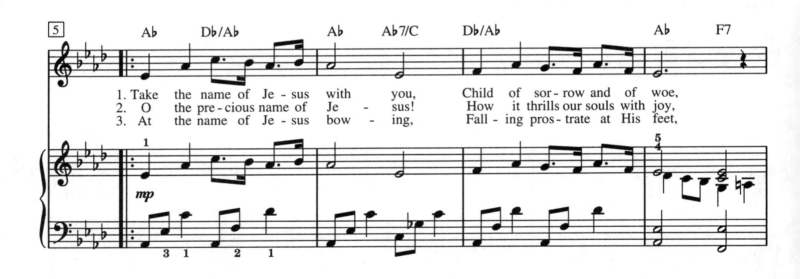

1. Take the name of Je-sus with you, Child of sor-row and of woe,
2. O the pre-cious name of Je - sus! How it thrills our souls with joy,
3. At the name of Je-sus bow - ing, Fall-ing pros-trate at His feet,

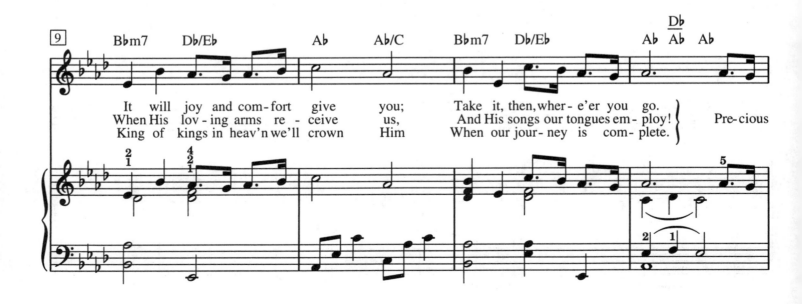

It will joy and com-fort give you; Take it, then, wher-e'er you go.
When His lov-ing arms re - ceive us, And His songs our tongues em-ploy!
King of kings in heav'n we'll crown Him When our jour-ney is com-plete.

Pre-cious

Joyful, Joyful, We Adore Thee

Words by Henry van Dyke

Music by Ludwig van Beethoven
Arranged by Jerry Ray

Not too fast–majestically

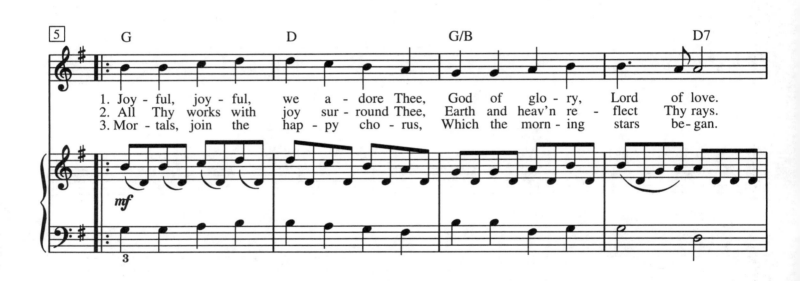

1. Joy - ful, joy - ful, we a - dore Thee, God of glo - ry, Lord of love.
2. All Thy works with joy sur - round Thee, Earth and heav'n re - flect Thy rays.
3. Mor - tals, join the hap - py cho - rus, Which the morn - ing stars be - gan.

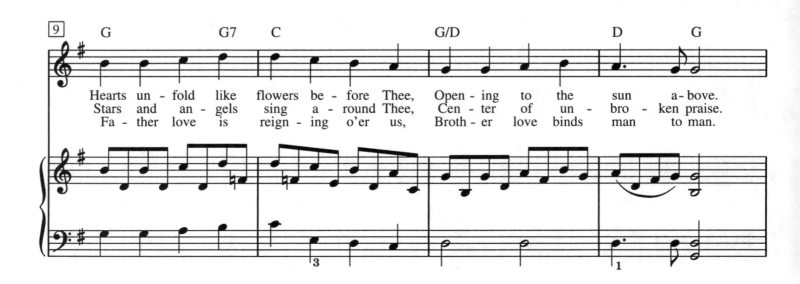

Hearts un - fold like flowers be - fore Thee, Open - ing to the sun a - bove.
Stars and an - gels sing a - round Thee, Cen - ter of un - bro - ken praise.
Fa - ther love is reign - ing o'er us, Broth - er love binds man to man.

My Faith Looks Up to Thee

Words by Ray Palmer

Music by Lowell Mason
Arranged by Jerry Ray

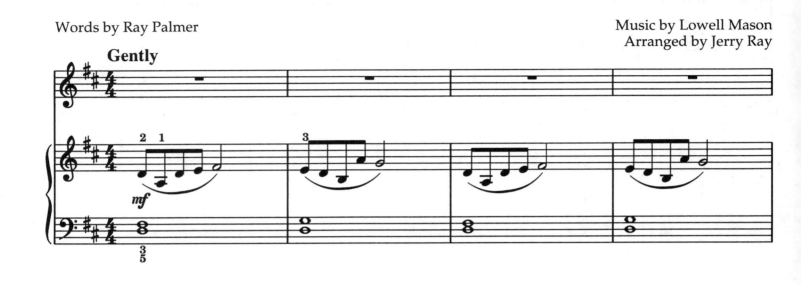

1. My faith looks up to Thee, Thou Lamb of
2. May Thy rich grace im - part Strength to my
3. When ends life's pass - ing dream, When death's cold,

Cal - va - ry, Sav - ior di - vine!
faint - ing heart, My zeal in - spire!
threat - 'ning stream Shall o'er me roll,

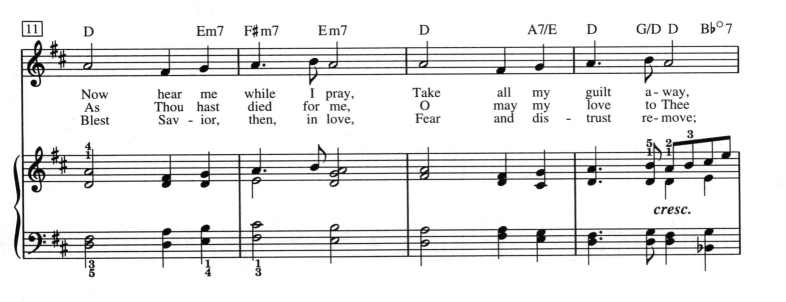

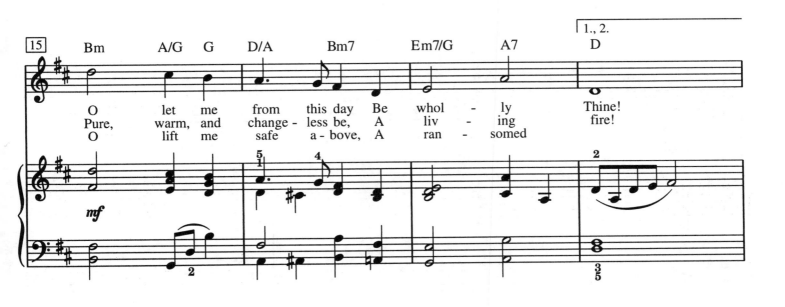

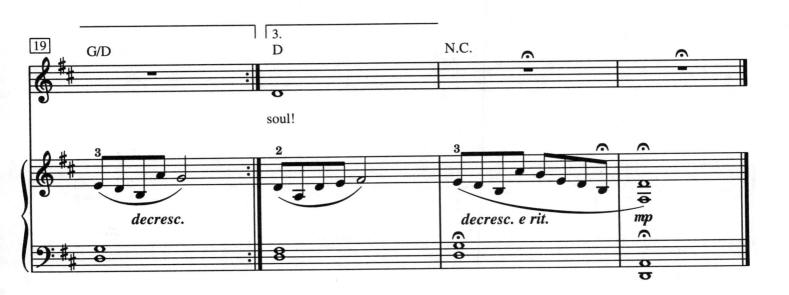

Pass Me Not

Words by Fanny J. Crosby

Music by William H. Doane
Arranged by Jerry Ray

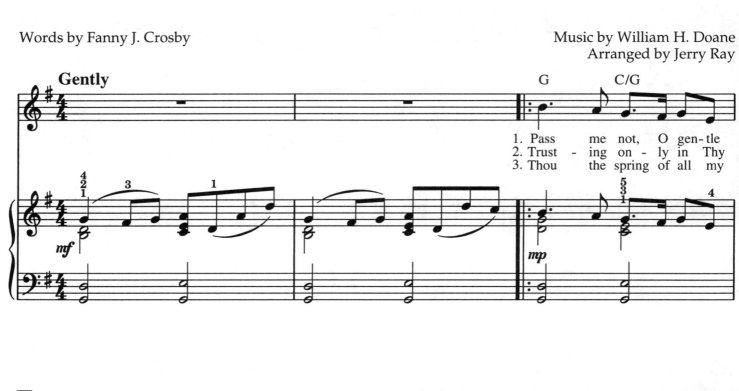

1. Pass me not, O gen-tle
2. Trust - ing on - ly in Thy
3. Thou the spring of all my

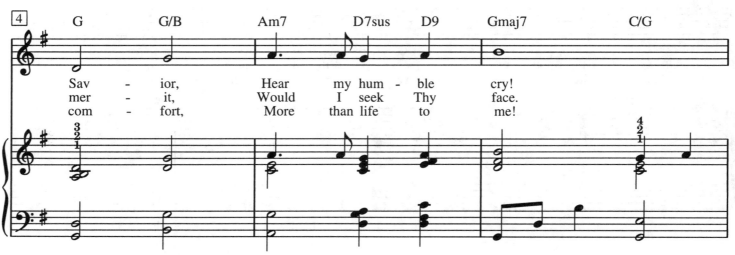

Sav - ior,   Hear my hum - ble cry!
mer - it,   Would I seek Thy face.
com - fort,   More than life to me!

While on oth - ers Thou art call - ing,   Do not pass me
Heal my wound - ed, bro - ken spir - it,   Save me by Thy
Whom have I on earth be - side Thee?   Whom in heav'n but

This Is My Father's World

Words by Maltbie D. Babcock

Music by Franklin L. Sheppard
Arranged by Jerry Ray

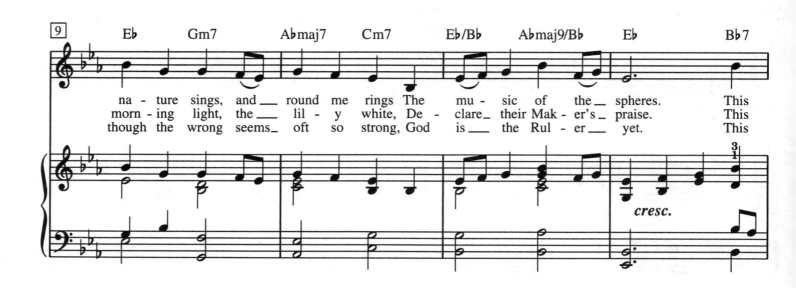

When the Roll Is Called Up Yonder

Words by James M. Black

Music by James M. Black
Arranged by Jerry Ray

1. When the trum-pet of the Lord shall sound and time shall be no more, And the
bright and cloud-less morn-ing when the dead in Christ shall rise, And the
la-bor for the Mas-ter from the dawn till set-ting sun, Let us

morn-ing breaks e - ter-nal, bright and fair;
glo-ry of His res - ur-rec-tion share;
talk of all His won-drous love and care;

When the saved of earth shall gath-er o - ver
When His cho-sen ones shall gath-er to their
Then when all of life is o - ver and our

Just As I Am

Words by Charlotte Elliott

Music by William B. Bradbury
Arranged by Jerry Ray

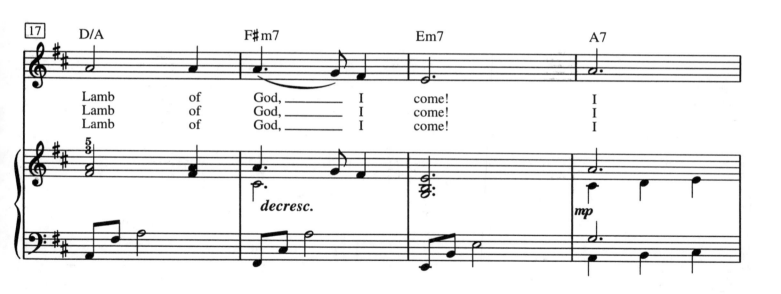

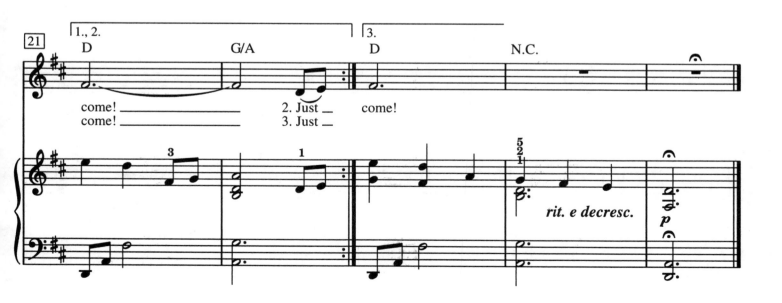

My Jesus, I Love Thee

Words by William R. Featherston

Music by Adoniram J. Gordon
Arranged by Jerry Ray

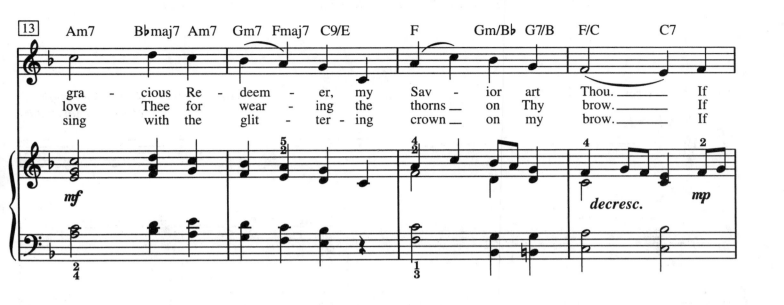

Praise to the Lord, the Almighty

Words by Joachim Neander

Music from *"Stralsund Gesangbuch"*
Arranged by Jerry Ray

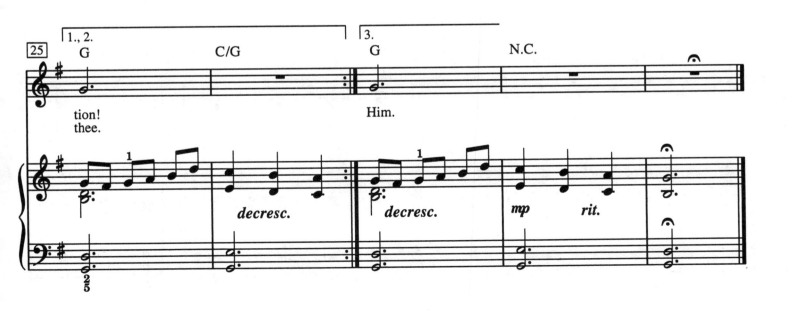

Beneath the Cross of Jesus

Words by Elizabeth C. Clephane

Music by Frederick C. Maker
Arranged by Jerry Ray

For the Beauty of the Earth

Words by Folliott S. Pierpoint

Music by Conrad Kocher
Arranged by Jerry Ray

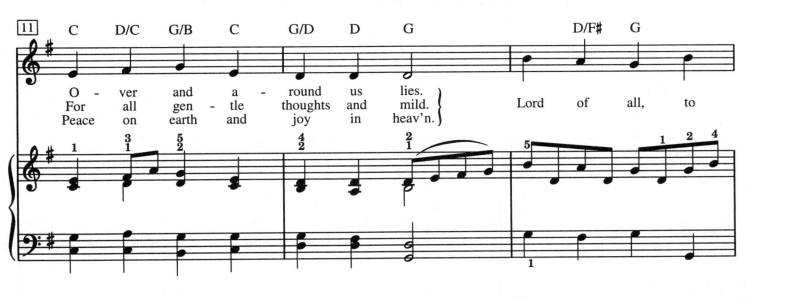

Over and around us lies.
For all gentle thoughts and mild.
Peace on earth and joy in heav'n.
Lord of all, to

Thee we raise This our hymn of grateful praise. grateful praise.

In the Sweet By and By

Words by S. F. Bennett

Music by J. P. Webster
Arranged by Jerry Ray

1. There's a

land that is fair - er than day, And by faith we can see it a -
sing on that beau - ti - ful shore The me - lo - di - ous songs of the
boun - ti - ful Fa - ther a - bove We will of - fer the trib - ute of

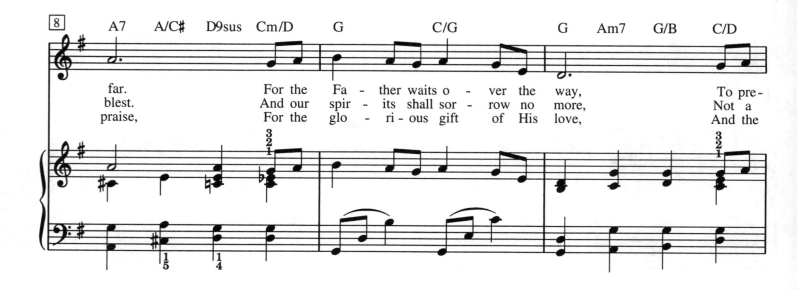

far. For the Fa - ther waits o - ver the way, To pre-
blest. And our spir - its shall sor - row no more, Not a
praise, For the glo - ri - ous gift of His love, And the

Revive Us Again

. Mackay

Music by John J. Husband
Arranged by Jerry Ray

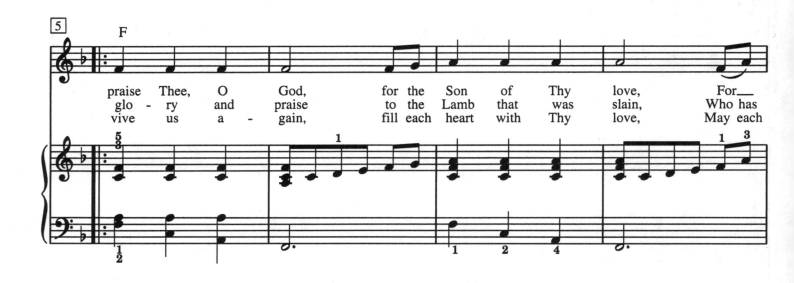

Stand Up, Stand Up for Jesus

Words by George Duffield, Jr.

Music by George J. Webb
Arranged by Jerry Ray

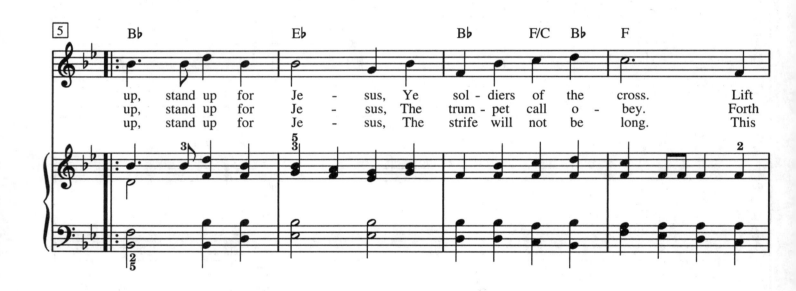

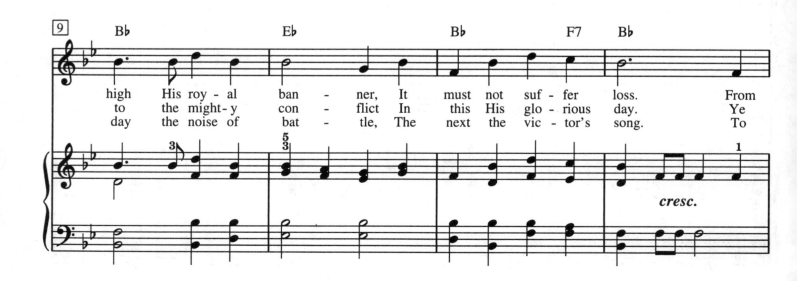

Thou Wilt Keep Him in Perfect Peace

Words by Vivian Kretz

Music by Vivian Kretz
Arranged by Jerry Ray

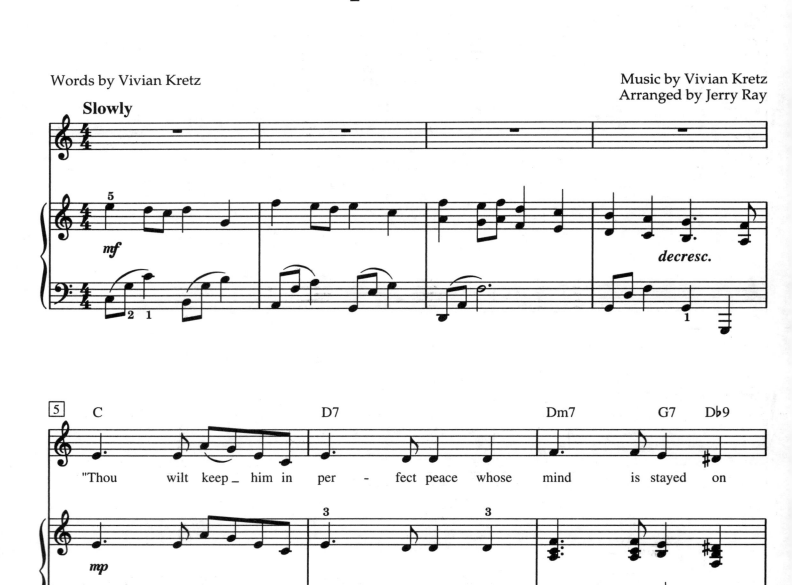

May Jesus Christ Be Praised

(When Morning Gilds the Skies)

Words translated by Edward Caswall

Music by Joseph Barnby
Arranged by Jerry Ray

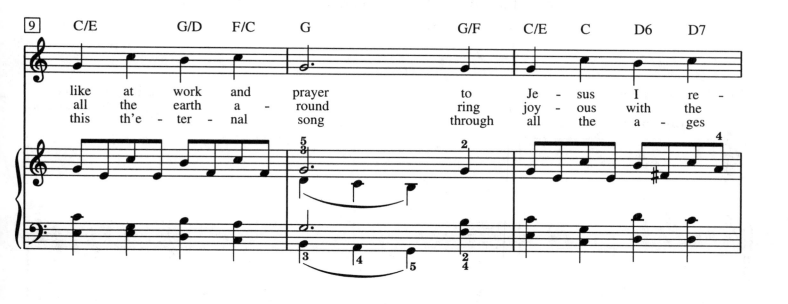

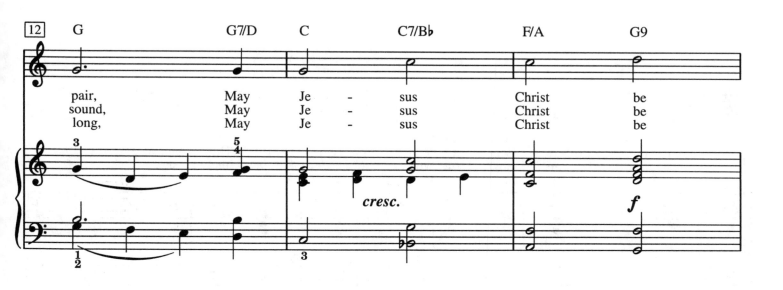

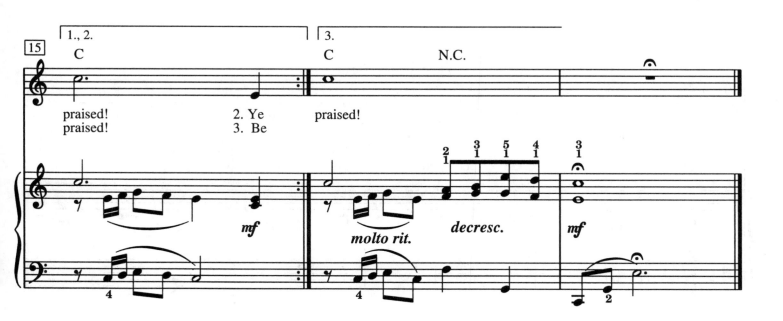

Nearer, My God, to Thee

Words by Sarah F. Adams

Music by Lowell Mason
Arranged by Jerry Ray

Moderately

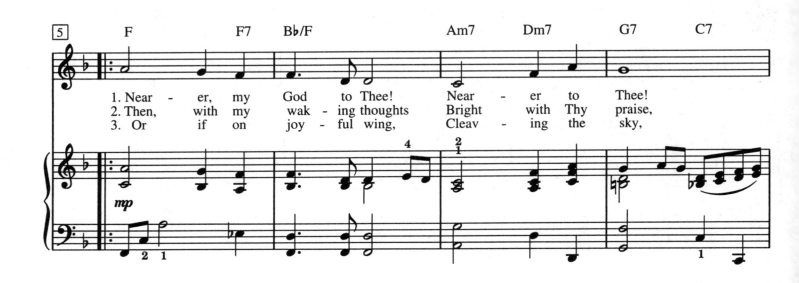

1. Near - er, my God to Thee! Near - er to Thee!
2. Then, with my wak - ing thoughts Bright with Thy praise,
3. Or if on joy - ful wing, Cleav - ing the sky,

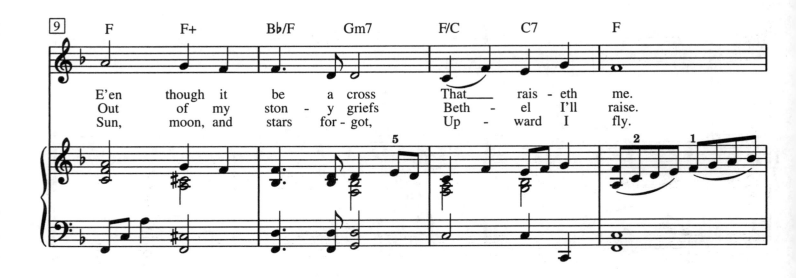

E'en though it be a cross That___ rais - eth me.
Out of my ston - y griefs Beth - el I'll raise.
Sun, moon, and stars for - got, Up - ward I fly.

Blessed Assurance

Words by Fanny J. Crosby

Music by Phoebe P. Knapp
Arranged by Jerry Ray

Near to the Heart of God

Words by Cleland B. McAfee

Music by Cleland B. McAfee
Arranged by Jerry Ray

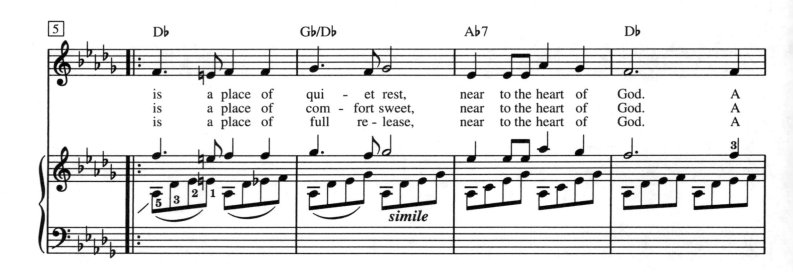

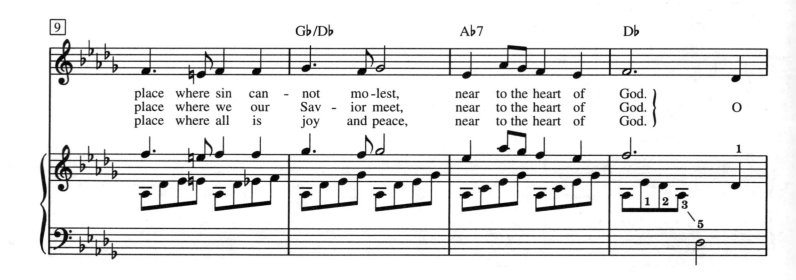

Take My Life and Let It Be

Words by Frances Ridley Havergal

Music by Henry A. César Malan
Arranged by Jerry Ray

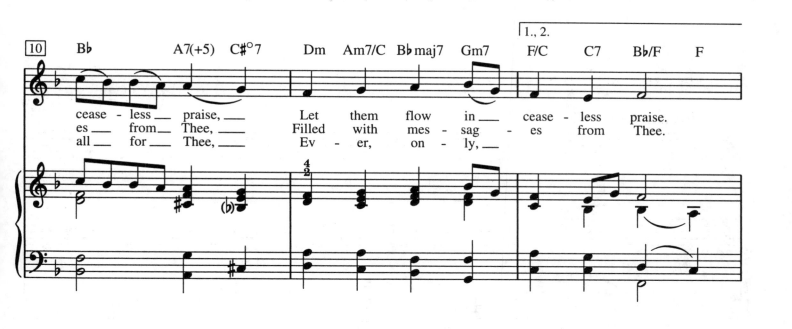

cease - less __ praise, __ Let them flow in __ cease - less praise.
es __ from __ Thee, __ Filled with mes - sag - es from Thee.
all __ for __ Thee, __ Ev - er, on - ly, __

all for Thee.

He Leadeth Me

Words by Joseph Gilmore

Music by William B. Bradbury
Arranged by Jerry Ray

Blest Be the Tie That Binds

Words by John Fawcett

Music by Johann G. Näegeli
Arranged by Jerry Ray

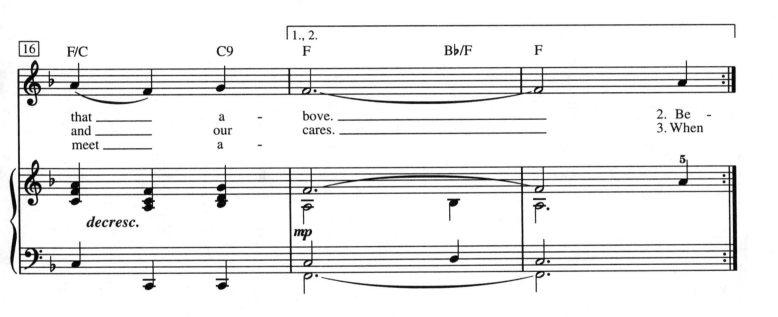

Rock of Ages

Words by Augustus M. Toplady

Music by Thomas Hastings
Arranged by Jerry Ray

sin the dou - ble cure, Cleanse me from its guilt and
to the foun - tain fly, Wash me, Sav - ior, or I
A - ges, cleft for me, Let me hide my - self in

pow'r.
die!
2. Noth - ing Thee.
3. While I

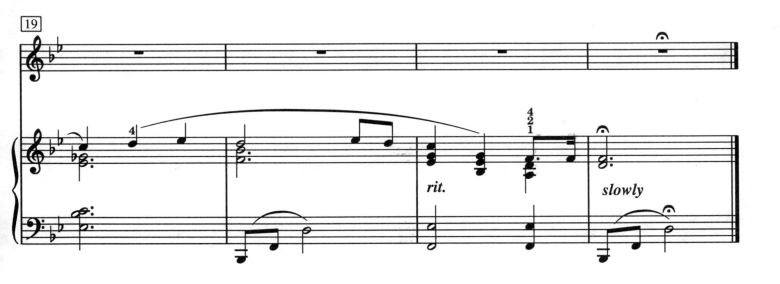

rit. *slowly*

Sweet Hour of Prayer

Words by William W. Walford

Music by William B. Bradbury
Arranged by Jerry Ray

What a Friend We Have in Jesus

Words by Joseph M. Scriven

Music by Charles C. Converse
Arranged by Jerry Ray

1. What a Friend we have in Je - sus, all our sins and griefs to bear!
2. Have we tri - als and temp - ta - tions? Is there trou - ble an - y - where?
3. Are we weak and heav - y - lad - en, cum - bered with a load of care?

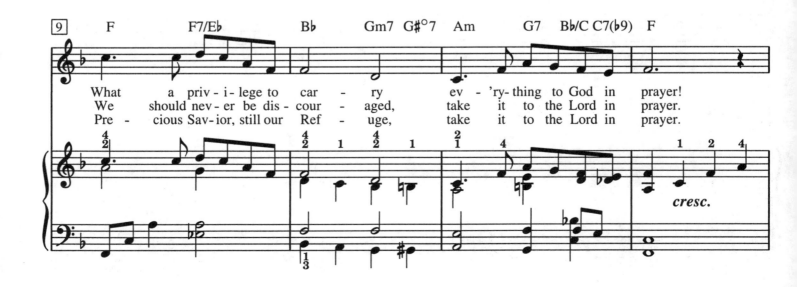

What a priv - i - lege to car - ry ev - 'ry - thing to God in prayer!
We should nev - er be dis - cour - aged, take it to the Lord in prayer.
Pre - cious Sav - ior, still our Ref - uge, take it to the Lord in prayer.

Were You There?

Traditional Spiritual
Arranged by Jerry Ray

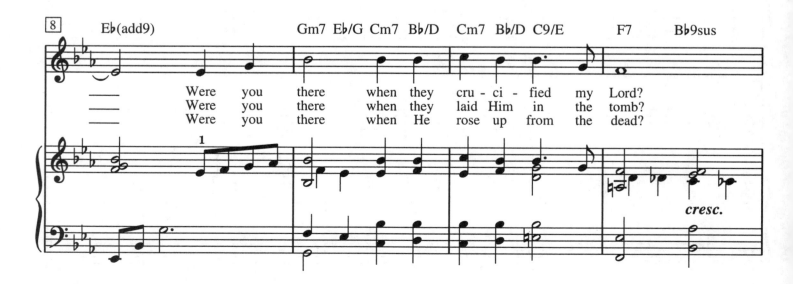

When I Survey the Wondrous Cross

Words by Isaac Watts

Based on a Gregorian Chant
Arranged by Jerry Ray

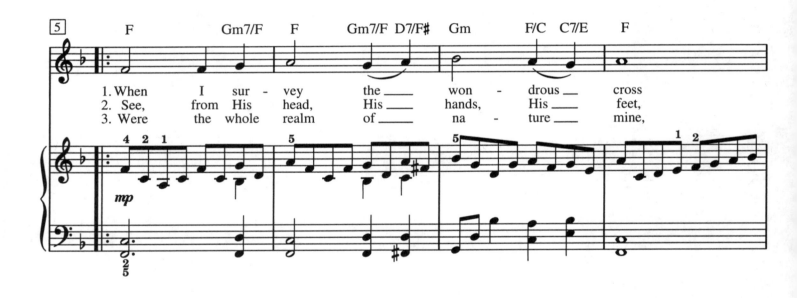

1. When I sur - vey the ___ won - drous ___ cross
2. See, from His head, His ___ hands, His ___ feet,
3. Were the whole realm of ___ na - ture ___ mine,

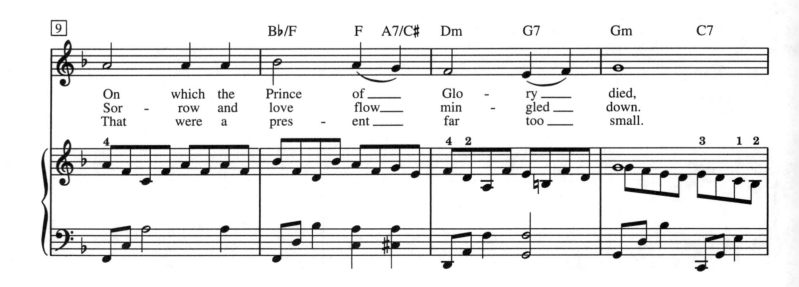

On which the Prince of ___ Glo - ry ___ died,
Sor - row and love flow ___ min - gled ___ down.
That were a pres - ent ___ far too ___ small.

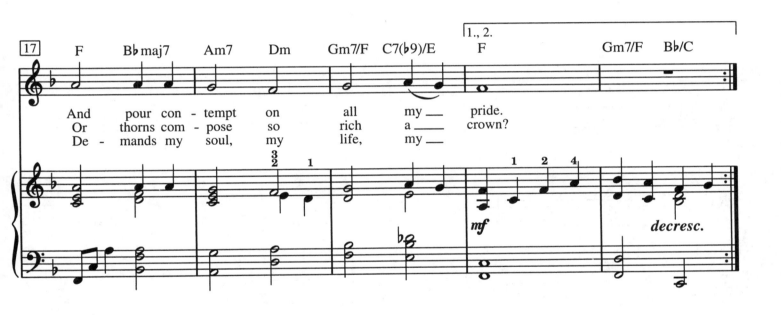

Come, Thou Long-Expected Jesus

Words by Charles Wesley

Music by Rowland H. Prichard
Arranged by Jerry Ray

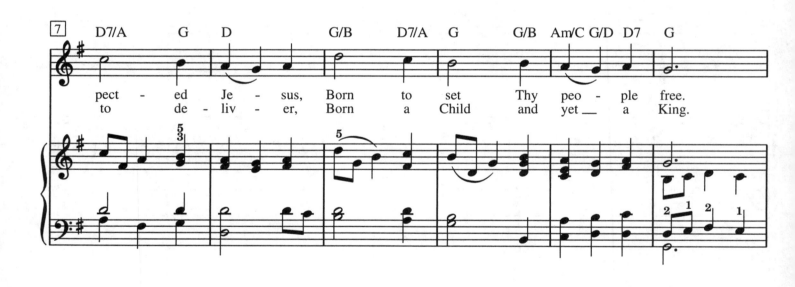

His Eye Is on the Sparrow

Words by Civilla D. Martin

Music by Charles H. Gabriel
Arranged by Jerry Ray

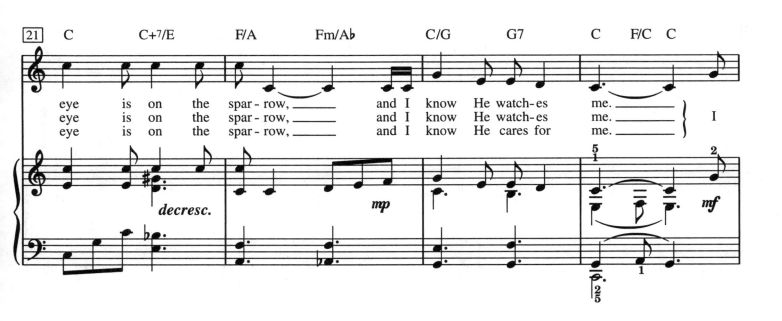

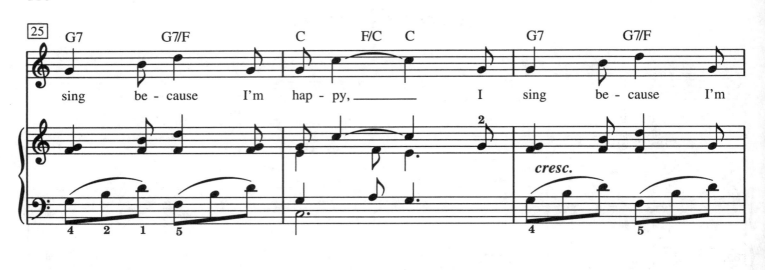

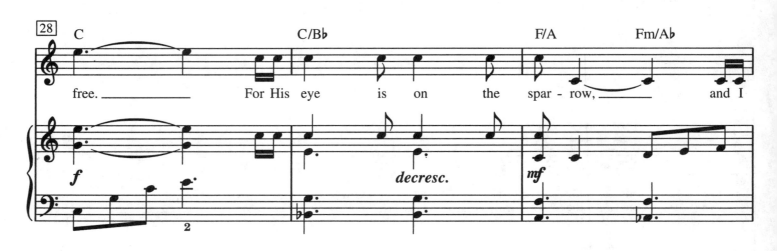

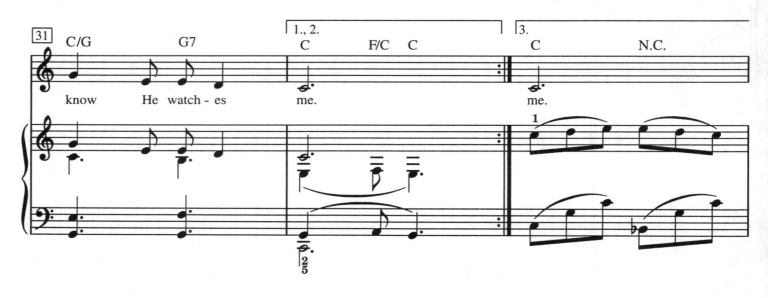

In the Garden

Words by C. Austin Miles

Music by C. Austin Miles
Arranged by Jerry Ray

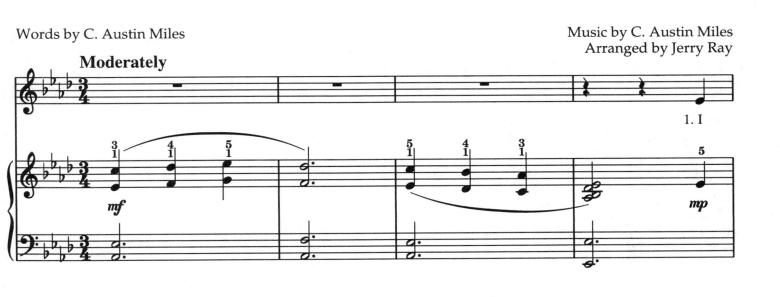

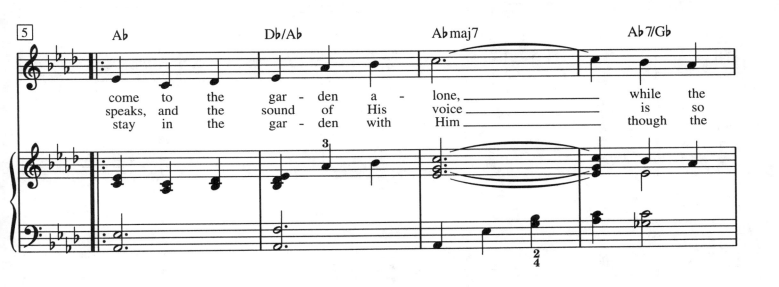

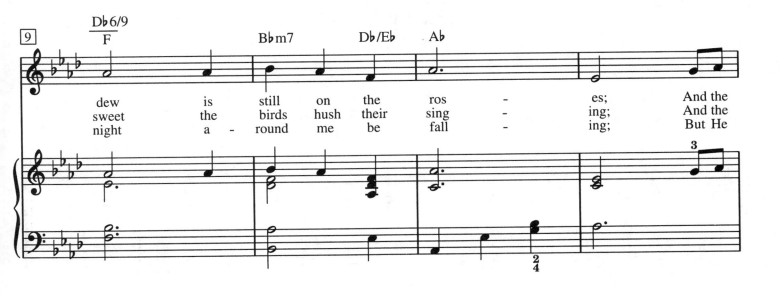

O God, Our Help in Ages Past

Words by Isaac Watts

Music by William Croft
Arranged by Jerry Ray

1. O

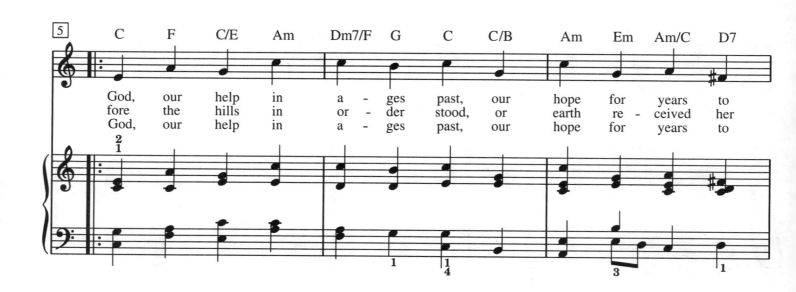

God, our help in a - ges past, our hope for years to
fore the hills in or - der stood, or earth re - ceived her
God, our help in a - ges past, our hope for years to

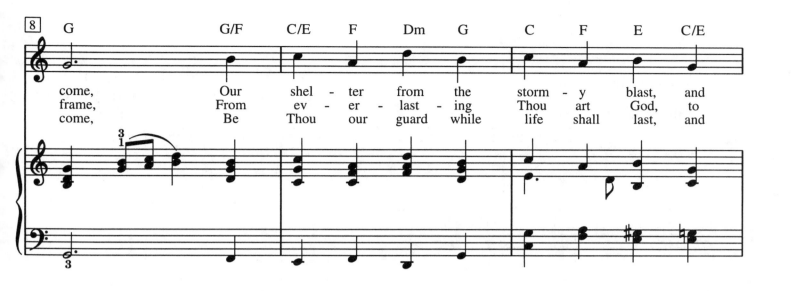

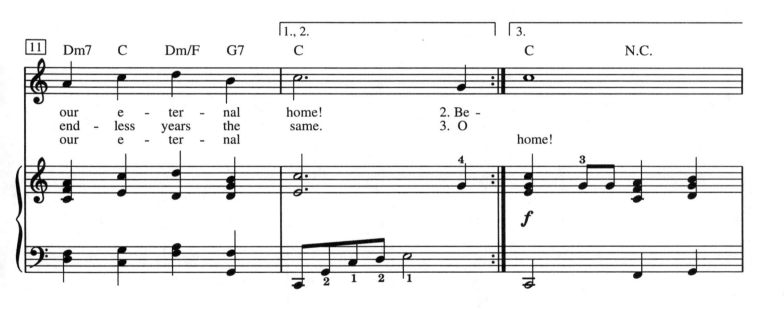

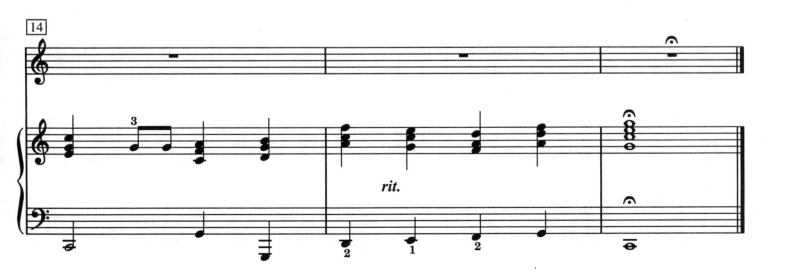

Jesus Is All the World to Me

Words by Will L. Thompson

Music by Will L. Thompson
Arranged by Jerry Ray

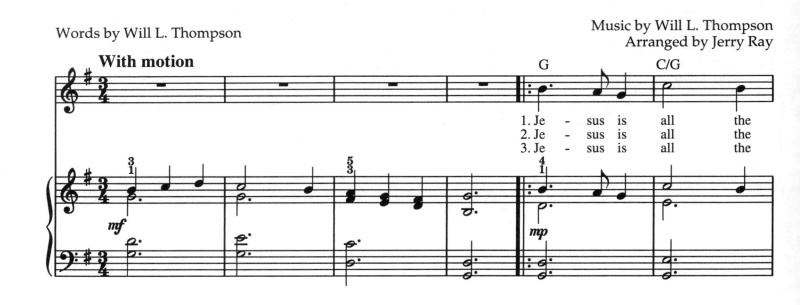

1. Je - sus is all the world to me, my life, my joy, my all._____ He
2. Je - sus is all the world to me, my Friend in tri - als sore._____ I
3. Je - sus is all the world to me, I want no bet - ter friend._____ I

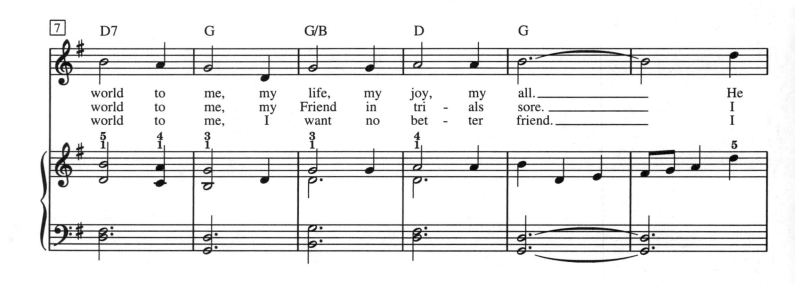

is my strength from day to day, with - out Him I____ would
go to Him for bless - ings, and He gives them o'er ____ and
trust Him now, I'll trust Him when life's fleet - ing days ____ shall

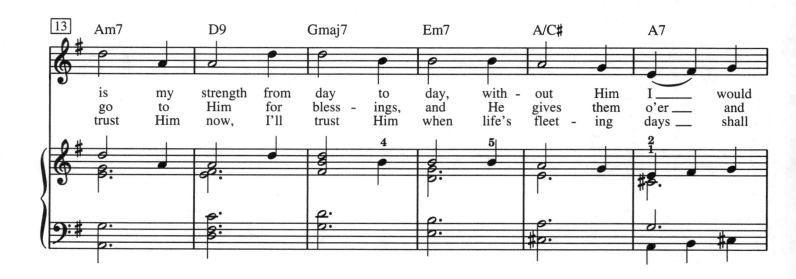

The Old Rugged Cross

Words by George Bennard

Music by George Bennard
Arranged by Jerry Ray

1. On a hill far a - way stood an old rug-ged cross, the em - blem of suf - f'ring and shame. _____

old rug-ged cross, so de - spised by the world, has a won - drous at - trac - tion for me. _____

old rug-ged cross I will ev - er be true, its shame and re - proach glad - ly bear. _____

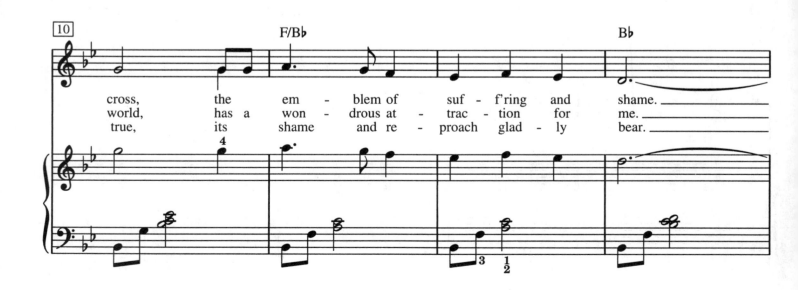

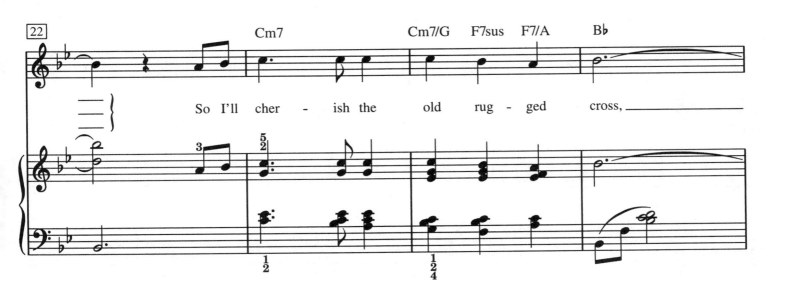

Just a Closer Walk with Thee

Traditional Folk Song
Arranged by Jerry Ray

Moment by Moment

Words by Daniel W. Whittle

Music by May Whittle Moody
Arranged by Jerry Ray

Not too fast

1. Dy - ing with Je - sus, by death reck-oned mine; Liv - ing with Je - sus a new life di - vine; Look - ing to Je - sus till glo - ry doth shine. Mo - ment by mo - ment, O

2. Nev - er a tri - al that He is not there; Nev - er a bur - den that He doth not bear; Nev - er a sor - row that He doth not share. Mo - ment by mo - ment, I'm

3. Nev - er a weak - ness that He doth not feel; Nev - er a sick - ness that He can - not heal; Mo - ment by mo - ment, in woe or in weal, Je - sus my Sav - ior a -

Softly and Tenderly

Words by Will L. Thompson

Music by Will L. Thompson
Arranged by Jerry Ray

Onward, Christian Soldiers

Words by Sabine Baring-Gould

Music by Arthur S. Sullivan
Arranged by Jerry Ray

1. On - ward, Chris - tian sol - diers, march - ing as to war,
2. Like a might - y ar - my moves the Church of God.
3. On - ward, then, ye peo - ple, join our hap - py throng.

With the cross of Je - sus go - ing on be - fore!
Broth - ers, we are tread - ing where the saints have trod.
Blend with ours your voic - es, in the tri - umph song.

Christ, the roy - al Mas - ter, leads a - gainst the foe;
We are not di - vid - ed, all one bod - y we,
Glo - ry, laud and hon - or un - to Christ the King,

Praise Him! Praise Him!

Words by Fanny J. Crosby

Music by Chester G. Allen
Arranged by Jerry Ray

Praise Him! praise Him! Je - sus, our bless - ed Re - deem - er!

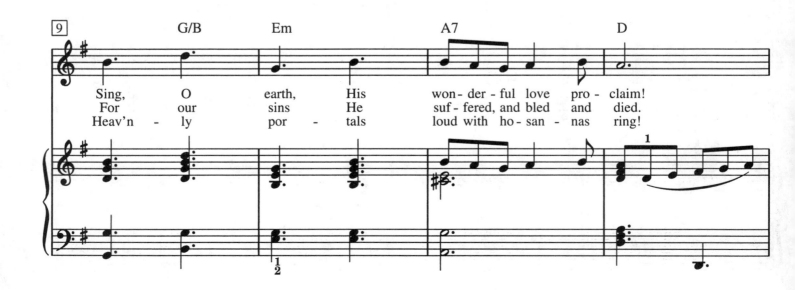

Sing,   O   earth,   His   won - der - ful love pro - claim!
For   our   sins   He   suf - fered, and bled   and died.
Heav'n - ly   por -   tals loud with ho - san - nas ring!

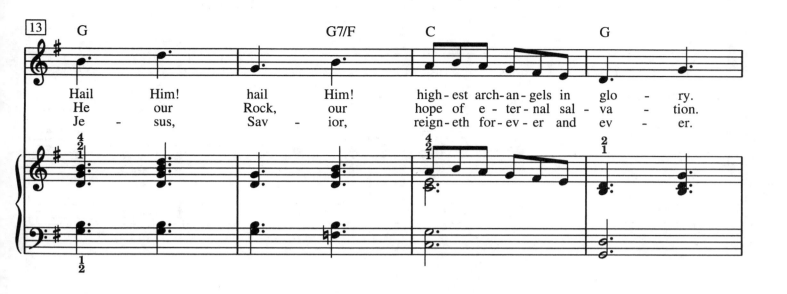

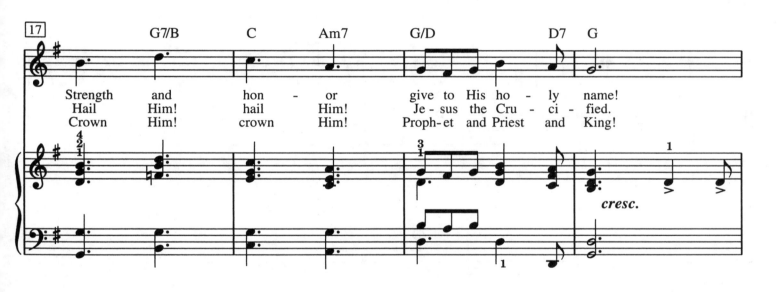

I Love to Tell the Story

Words by A. Catherine Hankey

Music by William G. Fischer
Arranged by Jerry Ray

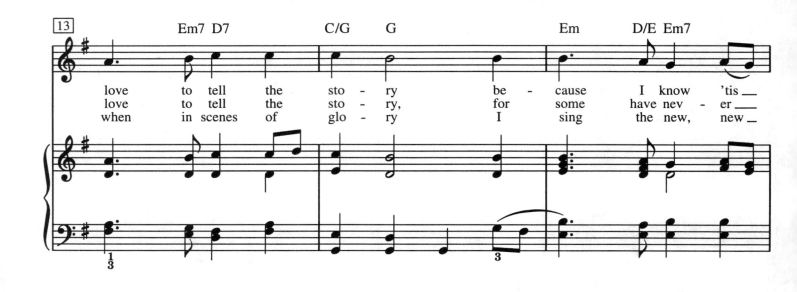

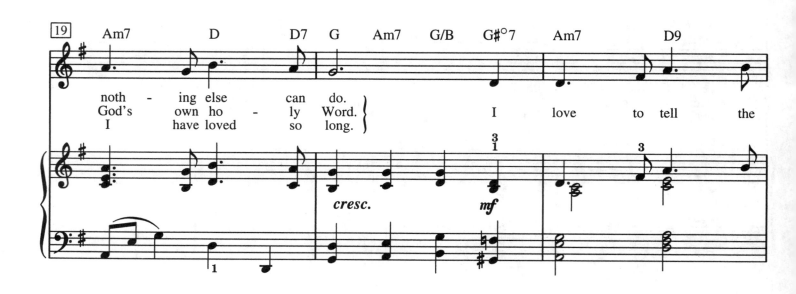

It Is Well with My Soul

Words by Horatio G. Spafford

Music by Philip P. Bliss
Arranged by Jerry Ray

Be Still, My Soul

Words by Katharina von Schlegel
Translated by Jane L. Borthwick

Music by Jean Sibelius
Arranged by Jerry Ray

1. Be still, my soul, the Lord is on thy side; ___
2. Be still, my soul, thy God doth un - der - take ___
3. Be still, my soul, the hour is has - tening on ___

Bear pa - tient - ly the cross of grief or pain.
To guide the fu - ture as He has the past.
When we shall be for - ev - er with the Lord.

Leave to thy God to or - der and pro - vide. ___
Thy hope, thy con - fi - dence let noth - ing shake. ___
When dis - ap - point - ment, grief, and fear are gone, ___

Near the Cross

Words by Fanny J. Crosby

Music by William H. Doane
Arranged by Jerry Ray

1. Je - sus, keep me near the cross, there a pre - cious foun - tain, Free to all, a heal - ing stream, flows from Cal - v'ry's
2. Near the cross! O Lamb of God, bring its scenes be - fore me. Help my walk from day to day with its shad - ows
3. Near the cross I'll watch and wait, hop - ing, trust - ing ev - er. Till I reach the gold - en strand just be - yond the

God of Our Fathers

Words by Daniel C. Roberts

Music by George W. Warren
Arranged by Jerry Ray

Lyrics:

1. God of our fa - thers, whose al - might - y hand Leads forth in beau - ty all the star - ry band Of shin - ing worlds in
2. Thy love di - vine hath led us in the past, In this free land by Thee our lot is cast. Be Thou our Rul - er,
3. Re - fresh Thy peo - ple on their toil - some way, Lead us from night to nev - er - end - ing day. Fill all our lives with

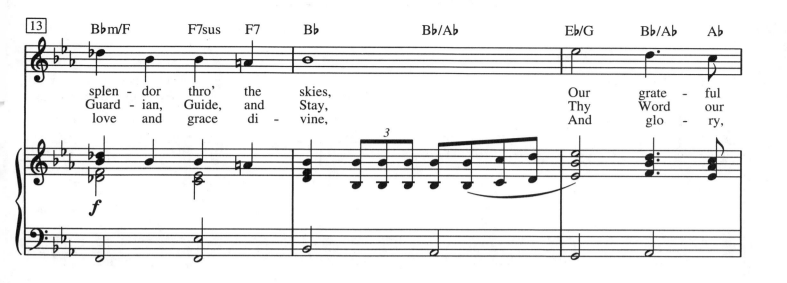

Kum Ba Yah

Traditional African Song
Arranged by Jerry Ray